WHITE STURGEON

You may have caught some lunkers in your time, but the likely North American record is in a different league. Let's put it this way: If you had hooked it from a fishing kayak, you'd have needed a bigger boat. The White Sturgeon (which was measured, then released) was 11 feet, 2 inches long and likely weighed half a ton. While the record is unofficial (as the fish was released), the photos don't lie. If you want to try your luck, head to the Fraser River in British Columbia, where the fish was caught.

SPECIES: _____ DATE: _____

LOCATION: _____

BAIT: _____

NOTES: _____

_____

_____

_____

SPECIES: _____ DATE: _____

LOCATION: _____

BAIT: _____

NOTES: _____

_____

_____

_____

SPECIES: _____ DATE: _____

LOCATION: _____

BAIT: _____

NOTES: _____

_____

_____

_____

SPECIES: _____ DATE: _____

LOCATION: _____

BAIT: _____

NOTES: _____

_____

_____

_____

THE FISH LEAD A PLEASANT LIFE: THEY DRINK WHEN THEY LIKE.

– German proverb

SPECIES: DATE:

LOCATION:

BAIT:

NOTES:

SPECIES: DATE:

LOCATION:

BAIT:

NOTES:

SPECIES: DATE:

LOCATION:

BAIT:

NOTES:

SPECIES: DATE:

LOCATION:

BAIT:

NOTES:

SPECIES: DATE:

LOCATION:

BAIT:

NOTES:

SPECIES: _____ DATE: _____

LOCATION: _____

BAIT: _____

NOTES: _____

_____

_____

_____

SPECIES: _____ DATE: _____

LOCATION: _____

BAIT: _____

NOTES: _____

_____

_____

_____

SPECIES: _____ DATE: _____

LOCATION: _____

BAIT: _____

NOTES: _____

_____

_____

_____

SPECIES: _____ DATE: _____

LOCATION: _____

BAIT: _____

NOTES: _____

_____

_____

_____

SPECIES: _____ DATE: _____

LOCATION: _____

BAIT: _____

NOTES: _____

_____

_____

_____

SPECIES: _____ DATE: _____

LOCATION: _____

BAIT: _____

NOTES: _____

_____

_____

_____

SPECIES: _____ DATE: _____

LOCATION: _____

BAIT: _____

NOTES: _____

_____

_____

_____

SPECIES: _____ DATE: _____

LOCATION: _____

BAIT: _____

NOTES: _____

_____

_____

_____

SPECIES: _____ DATE: _____

LOCATION: _____

BAIT: _____

NOTES: _____

_____

_____

_____

SPECIES: _____ DATE: _____

LOCATION: _____

BAIT: _____

NOTES: _____

_____

_____

_____

NORTHERN PIKE

This fast, hard-fighting sight-predator is famous for its sudden attacks—the kind that can make a bobber disappear in a flash. The world record northern pike was caught in Germany in 1986 and was 50 pounds, 1 ounce. But northern pike shouldn't be overlooked as table fare; while they are infamously bony, the bones can be removed via a technique called Y-boning. This removes a long section of Y-shaped bones that run along the center of the fish. Once these are removed, you've got a bone-free fillet. Note: This takes some practice, and you'll need a sharp knife, but there are plenty of how-tos on YouTube and Google!

SPECIES: _____ DATE: _____

LOCATION: _____

BAIT: _____

NOTES: _____

_____

_____

_____

SPECIES: _____ DATE: _____

LOCATION: _____

BAIT: _____

NOTES: _____

_____

_____

_____

SPECIES: _____ DATE: _____

LOCATION: _____

BAIT: _____

NOTES: _____

_____

_____

_____

SPECIES: _____ DATE: _____

LOCATION: _____

BAIT: _____

NOTES: _____

_____

_____

_____

SPECIES: _____ DATE: _____

LOCATION: _____

BAIT: _____

NOTES: _____

_____

_____

_____

SPECIES: _____ DATE: _____

LOCATION: _____

BAIT: _____

NOTES: _____

_____

_____

_____

SPECIES: _____ DATE: _____

LOCATION: _____

BAIT: _____

NOTES: _____

_____

_____

_____

SPECIES: _____ DATE: _____

LOCATION: _____

BAIT: _____

NOTES: _____

_____

_____

_____

SPECIES: _____ DATE: _____

LOCATION: _____

BAIT: _____

NOTES: _____

_____

_____

_____

SPECIES: _____ DATE: _____

LOCATION: _____

BAIT: _____

NOTES: _____

_____

_____

_____

SPECIES: _____ DATE: _____

LOCATION: _____

BAIT: _____

NOTES: _____

_____

_____

SPECIES: _____ DATE: _____

LOCATION: _____

BAIT: _____

NOTES: _____

_____

_____

SPECIES: _____ DATE: _____

LOCATION: _____

BAIT: _____

NOTES: _____

_____

_____

SPECIES: _____ DATE: _____

LOCATION: _____

BAIT: _____

NOTES: _____

_____

_____

SPECIES: _____ DATE: _____

LOCATION: _____

BAIT: _____

NOTES: _____

_____

_____

SPECIES: DATE:

LOCATION:

BAIT:

NOTES:

SPECIES: DATE:

LOCATION:

BAIT:

NOTES:

SPECIES: DATE:

LOCATION:

BAIT:

NOTES:

SPECIES: DATE:

LOCATION:

BAIT:

NOTES:

SPECIES: DATE:

LOCATION:

BAIT:

NOTES:

TARPON

When it comes to saltwater fishing, tarpon are certainly among the most popular sportfish. Famous for their acrobatic leaps and fighting ability, tarpon also reach incredible sizes. In Florida, the state record (on conventional fishing gear) is an amazing 243 pounds. Some anglers opt to catch them on fly-fishing gear—which is often quite light-weight, making for tremendous, long-running battles—and plenty of fish that jump off the hook. The world record for a tarpon on fly-fishing gear was set in 2000, and the fish weighed just over 202 pounds. Because tarpon are not good table fare, nearly all tarpon anglers practice catch-and-release.

SPECIES: DATE:

LOCATION:

BAIT:

NOTES:

SPECIES: DATE:

LOCATION:

BAIT:

NOTES:

WALLEYE

The Walleye is among the most sought-after sportfish in the northern reaches of the country. The state fish of three different U.S. states—Minnesota, South Dakota, and Vermont—it's also the provincial fish of Manitoba and Saskatchewan. Famous for its great taste (it's often considered one of the best-tasting freshwater fish), walleye has a devoted following among anglers. That fanbase even spills over into municipalities throughout the north, where there are a number of huge fiberglass statues in homage to walleyes; examples include those in Baudette, Minnesota; Garrison, Minnesota; and Garrison, South Dakota. Ice fishing for walleye is especially popular, with some walleye lakes practically carpeted with ice houses. You can fish in comfort, too, as permanent ice houses (they stay on the lake throughout the winter) can have heat, beds, and, sometimes, even full bars.

SPECIES: _____ DATE: _____

LOCATION: _____

BAIT: _____

NOTES: _____

_____

_____

_____

SPECIES: _____ DATE: _____

LOCATION: _____

BAIT: _____

NOTES: _____

_____

_____

_____

SPECIES: _____ DATE: _____

LOCATION: _____

BAIT: _____

NOTES: _____

_____

_____

_____

SPECIES: _____ DATE: _____

LOCATION: _____

BAIT: _____

NOTES: _____

_____

_____

_____

SPECIES: _____ DATE: _____

LOCATION: _____

BAIT: _____

NOTES: _____

_____

_____

_____

SPECIES: _____ DATE: _____

LOCATION: _____

BAIT: _____

NOTES: _____

_____

_____

_____

SPECIES: DATE:

LOCATION:

BAIT:

NOTES:

SPECIES: DATE:

LOCATION:

BAIT:

NOTES:

SPECIES: DATE:

LOCATION:

BAIT:

NOTES:

SPECIES: DATE:

LOCATION:

BAIT:

NOTES:

SPECIES: DATE:

LOCATION:

BAIT:

NOTES:

SPECIES: _____ DATE: _____

LOCATION: _____

BAIT: _____

NOTES: _____

_____

_____

SPECIES: _____ DATE: _____

LOCATION: _____

BAIT: _____

NOTES: _____

_____

_____

SPECIES: _____ DATE: _____

LOCATION: _____

BAIT: _____

NOTES: _____

_____

_____

SPECIES: _____ DATE: _____

LOCATION: _____

BAIT: _____

NOTES: _____

_____

_____

SPECIES: _____ DATE: _____

LOCATION: _____

BAIT: _____

NOTES: _____

_____

_____

SPECIES: DATE:

LOCATION:

BAIT:

NOTES:

SPECIES: DATE:

LOCATION:

BAIT:

NOTES:

SPECIES: DATE:

LOCATION:

BAIT:

NOTES:

SPECIES: DATE:

LOCATION:

BAIT:

NOTES:

SPECIES: DATE:

LOCATION:

BAIT:

NOTES:

LARGEMOUTH BASS

A wildly popular game fish, the largemouth bass is a hard-fighting fish famed for its wild leaps from the water and its voracious appetite—they'll sometimes even eat baby birds or practically anything else they can fit in their mouths. As its name suggests, the largemouth bass has a larger jaw than that of its smaller cousin, the smallmouth bass; the largemouth's jaw extends out past its orbital (eye) bone. The smallmouth's jaw only extends halfway to the middle of the eye. Largemouth bass are also larger than smallmouths—the record U.S. largemouth topped out at just over 22 pounds. Widely introduced, largemouth bass are now invasive in some areas where their appetite and size make them sometimes unwanted guests.

SPECIES: _____ DATE: _____

LOCATION: _____

BAIT: _____

NOTES: _____

_____

_____

_____

SPECIES: _____ DATE: _____

LOCATION: _____

BAIT: _____

NOTES: _____

_____

_____

_____

SPECIES: _____ DATE: _____

LOCATION: _____

BAIT: _____

NOTES: _____

_____

_____

_____

SPECIES: _____ DATE: _____

LOCATION: _____

BAIT: _____

NOTES: _____

_____

> # A MAN MAY FISH WITH THE WORM THAT HATH EAT OF A KING, AND EAT OF THE FISH THAT HATH FED OF THAT WORM.
>
> *– Hamlet*

SPECIES: _____ DATE: _____

LOCATION: _____

BAIT: _____

NOTES: _____

_____

_____

SPECIES: _____ DATE: _____

LOCATION: _____

BAIT: _____

NOTES: _____

_____

_____

SPECIES: _____ DATE: _____

LOCATION: _____

BAIT: _____

NOTES: _____

_____

_____

SPECIES: _____ DATE: _____

LOCATION: _____

BAIT: _____

NOTES: _____

_____

_____

SPECIES: _____ DATE: _____

LOCATION: _____

BAIT: _____

NOTES: _____

_____

_____

SPECIES: _____ DATE: _____

LOCATION: _____

BAIT: _____

NOTES: _____

_____

_____

_____

SPECIES: _____ DATE: _____

LOCATION: _____

BAIT: _____

NOTES: _____

_____

_____

_____

SMALLMOUTH BASS

They may be smaller than largemouth bass, but smallmouth bass are no less exciting to catch, as they often instinctively leap out of the water once hooked. What's more, smallies, as they are often known, also get quite large; record fish can reach up to almost 12 pounds, but even 5- or 6-pounders are considered trophy fish. As with largemouth bass, many smallmouth bass anglers practice catch-and-release in order to preserve trophy fish.

SPECIES: _____ DATE: _____

LOCATION: _____

BAIT: _____

NOTES: _____

_____

_____

_____

SPECIES: _____ DATE: _____

LOCATION: _____

BAIT: _____

NOTES: _____

_____

_____

_____

SPECIES: _____ DATE: _____

LOCATION: _____

BAIT: _____

NOTES: _____

_____

_____

_____

SPECIES: _____ DATE: _____

LOCATION: _____

BAIT: _____

NOTES: _____

_____

_____

_____

SPECIES: _____ DATE: _____

LOCATION: _____

BAIT: _____

NOTES: _____

_____

_____

_____

SPECIES: _____ DATE: _____

LOCATION: _____

BAIT: _____

NOTES: _____

_____

_____

_____

SPECIES: _____ DATE: _____

LOCATION: _____

BAIT: _____

NOTES: _____

_____

_____

_____

SPECIES: _____ DATE: _____

LOCATION: _____

BAIT: _____

NOTES: _____

_____

_____

_____

SPECIES: _____ DATE: _____

LOCATION: _____

BAIT: _____

NOTES: _____

_____

_____

_____

SPECIES: _____ DATE: _____

LOCATION: _____

BAIT: _____

NOTES: _____

_____

_____

_____

SPECIES: _____ DATE: _____

LOCATION: _____

BAIT: _____

NOTES: _____

_____

_____

_____

SPECIES: _____ DATE: _____

LOCATION: _____

BAIT: _____

NOTES: _____

_____

_____

_____

SPECIES: _____ DATE: _____

LOCATION: _____

BAIT: _____

NOTES: _____

_____

_____

_____

SPECIES: _____ DATE: _____

LOCATION: _____

BAIT: _____

NOTES: _____

_____

_____

_____

SPECIES: _____ DATE: _____

LOCATION: _____

BAIT: _____

NOTES: _____

_____

_____

_____

SPECIES: _____ DATE: _____

LOCATION: _____

BAIT: _____

NOTES: _____

_____

_____

_____

SPECIES: _____ DATE: _____

LOCATION: _____

BAIT: _____

NOTES: _____

_____

_____

_____

SPECIES: _____ DATE: _____

LOCATION: _____

BAIT: _____

NOTES: _____

_____

_____

_____

SPECIES: _____ DATE: _____

LOCATION: _____

BAIT: _____

NOTES: _____

_____

_____

_____

SPECIES: _____ DATE: _____

LOCATION: _____

BAIT: _____

NOTES: _____

_____

_____

_____

SPECIES: _____   DATE: _____

LOCATION: _____

BAIT: _____

NOTES: _____

_____

_____

SPECIES: _____   DATE: _____

LOCATION: _____

BAIT: _____

NOTES: _____

_____

_____

_____

CRAPPIES

Despite their odd name (it's pronounced CROP-ees), these are some of the most beloved panfish around. Two species of this member of the sunfish family are found in the U.S.— the black crappie, which is colored a speckled green and black, and the white crappie, which has a lighter complexion. Both species are revered as panfish, and they can put up a fight. And some crappies are absolute *slabs*; the all-time longest black crappie was an amazing 19 inches and weighed more than 5 pounds; the longest white crappie was about 14.5 inches long.

TUNA

Tuna are a group of related saltwater fish that are famous for their often huge size and great speed. Apex predators, they're found in deep water in oceans all around the world, including in many U.S. waters. There are more than a dozen tuna species, but you may recognize a few of the most sought-after varieties by their names alone: albacore, blackfin, yellowfin, and, of course, the Atlantic bluefin tuna, which can be absolutely massive; the record fish weighed 1,496 pounds. Unfortunately, large Atlantic bluefins have been dramatically overfished commercially, due in part to the extreme prices offered for individual fish. It's not unheard of for large fish—think 600 pounds—to go for hundreds of thousands of dollars—sometimes even millions—at auction. If you're wondering about the source of canned tuna: much of it comes from skipjack tuna, which is happily in much better shape, population-wise, than Atlantic bluefin tuna.

SPECIES: _____ DATE: _____

LOCATION: _____

BAIT: _____

NOTES: _____

_____

_____

SPECIES: _____ DATE: _____

LOCATION: _____

BAIT: _____

NOTES: _____

_____

_____

SPECIES: _____ DATE: _____

LOCATION: _____

BAIT: _____

NOTES: _____

_____

_____

SPECIES: _____ DATE: _____

LOCATION: _____

BAIT: _____

NOTES: _____

_____

_____

SPECIES: _____ DATE: _____

LOCATION: _____

BAIT: _____

NOTES: _____

_____

_____

SPECIES: _____ DATE: _____

LOCATION: _____

BAIT: _____

NOTES: _____

_____

_____

SPECIES: _____ DATE: _____

LOCATION: _____

BAIT: _____

NOTES: _____

_____

_____

SPECIES: _____ DATE: _____

LOCATION: _____

BAIT: _____

NOTES: _____

_____

_____

SPECIES: _____ DATE: _____

LOCATION: _____

BAIT: _____

NOTES: _____

_____

_____

SPECIES: _____ DATE: _____

LOCATION: _____

BAIT: _____

NOTES: _____

_____

_____

SPECIES: DATE:

LOCATION:

BAIT:

NOTES:

SPECIES: DATE:

LOCATION:

BAIT:

NOTES:

SPECIES: DATE:

LOCATION:

BAIT:

NOTES:

SPECIES: DATE:

LOCATION:

BAIT:

NOTES:

SPECIES: DATE:

LOCATION:

BAIT:

NOTES:

SPECIES: DATE:

LOCATION:

BAIT:

NOTES:

SPECIES: DATE:

LOCATION:

BAIT:

NOTES:

SPECIES: DATE:

LOCATION:

BAIT:

NOTES:

SPECIES: DATE:

LOCATION:

BAIT:

NOTES:

SPECIES: DATE:

LOCATION:

BAIT:

NOTES:

MUSKELLUNGE

Muskellunge, often referred to as "muskies," are one of the great freshwater trophy fish in North America. Minnesota, Michigan, Ontario, Wisconsin, and West Virginia are home to the prime muskie waters, though populations are scattered across a number of other states and provinces. Related to the northern pike, which can reach huge sizes itself, muskies get even bigger. Catching a 50-inch fish is considered a landmark in an angler's career, and muskies are known to attack almost anything in or near the water: birds, mammals, even other smaller muskies being reeled in by an angler. The world record, as recognized by the International Game Fish Association, was a 67-pound lunker caught in Wisconsin back in 1949. Intriguingly, Minnesota Department of Natural Resources staff caught an absolute monster fish while electrofishing on Mille Lacs lake, a noted muskie hotspot. They were unable to weigh the fish (as they didn't have a scale big enough to handle it), but they quickly measured it before releasing it. It was 61.5 inches long, which makes it longer (but not necessarily heavier) than the world record muskie.

SPECIES: DATE:

LOCATION:

BAIT:

NOTES:

SPECIES: DATE:

LOCATION:

BAIT:

NOTES:

SPECIES: DATE:

LOCATION:

BAIT:

NOTES:

SPECIES: DATE:

LOCATION:

BAIT:

NOTES:

SPECIES: DATE:

LOCATION:

BAIT:

NOTES:

SUNFISH

These plucky freshwater fish are a favorite of serious anglers, who revere them for their fight and how tasty they are, and they are beloved by kids, who like how easy they are to catch. Sunfish, especially bluegill and its close relatives (pumpkinseed, redears, and green sunfish), are native to wide swaths of the U.S. and have been introduced pretty much everywhere else. Sunfish size can range widely between each body of water, but they can get quite large. For example, in lakes known for bluegills, fish that are roughly dinner-plate size can occur. In other lakes, where fish are stunted, pesky "bait-robbers" prevail.

SPECIES: _____   DATE: _____

LOCATION: _____

BAIT: _____

NOTES: _____

_____

_____

_____

SPECIES: _____   DATE: _____

LOCATION: _____

BAIT: _____

NOTES: _____

_____

_____

_____

> # THE PERCH IS A DAINTIE FISH AND PASSING WHOLESOME FOR A MAN, HE IS ALSO A FREE AND GREEDY BYTER.
>
> – Leonard Mascall, *A Booke of Fishing with Hooke and Line* (1590)

SPECIES: _____ DATE: _____

LOCATION: _____

BAIT: _____

NOTES: _____

_____

_____

_____

SPECIES: _____ DATE: _____

LOCATION: _____

BAIT: _____

NOTES: _____

_____

_____

_____

SPECIES: _____ DATE: _____

LOCATION: _____

BAIT: _____

NOTES: _____

_____

_____

_____

SPECIES: _____ DATE: _____

LOCATION: _____

BAIT: _____

NOTES: _____

_____

_____

_____

SPECIES: _____ DATE: _____

LOCATION: _____

BAIT: _____

NOTES: _____

_____

_____

_____

SPECIES: _____ DATE: _____

LOCATION: _____

BAIT: _____

NOTES: _____

_____

_____

_____

SPECIES: _____ DATE: _____

LOCATION: _____

BAIT: _____

NOTES: _____

_____

_____

_____

SPECIES: _____ DATE: _____

LOCATION: _____

BAIT: _____

NOTES: _____

_____

_____

_____

SPECIES: _____ DATE: _____

LOCATION: _____

BAIT: _____

NOTES: _____

_____

_____

_____

SPECIES: DATE:

LOCATION:

BAIT:

NOTES:

SPECIES: DATE:

LOCATION:

BAIT:

NOTES:

SPECIES: DATE:

LOCATION:

BAIT:

NOTES:

SPECIES: DATE:

LOCATION:

BAIT:

NOTES:

SPECIES: DATE:

LOCATION:

BAIT:

NOTES:

YELLOW PERCH

Found throughout much of the U.S., these cousins to walleyes are some of the best table fare around. The trouble is, finding fish big enough to keep can prove difficult. It's pretty common to encounter many tiny yellow perch in an area, and they are often very proficient at stealing bait. But once you find fish that are no longer in the "nursery," you're in luck, as perch often school (for protection against predators) and so it's pretty common to catch similarly sized fish in succession. With that said, the true lunkers often strike out on their own, but even they can become prey. A large, fat perch may end up in your livewell, or in the belly of a large northern pike, walleye, or a muskellunge.

SPECIES: _____ DATE: _____

LOCATION: _____

BAIT: _____

NOTES: _____

_____

_____

SPECIES: _____ DATE: _____

LOCATION: _____

BAIT: _____

NOTES: _____

_____

_____

SPECIES: _____ DATE: _____

LOCATION: _____

BAIT: _____

NOTES: _____

_____

_____

SPECIES: _____ DATE: _____

LOCATION: _____

BAIT: _____

NOTES: _____

_____

_____

SPECIES: _____ DATE: _____

LOCATION: _____

BAIT: _____

NOTES: _____

_____

_____

SPECIES: _____ DATE: _____

LOCATION: _____

BAIT: _____

NOTES: _____

_____

_____

_____

SPECIES: _____ DATE: _____

LOCATION: _____

BAIT: _____

NOTES: _____

_____

_____

_____

SPECIES: _____ DATE: _____

LOCATION: _____

BAIT: _____

NOTES: _____

_____

_____

_____

SPECIES: _____ DATE: _____

LOCATION: _____

BAIT: _____

NOTES: _____

_____

_____

_____

SPECIES: _____ DATE: _____

LOCATION: _____

BAIT: _____

NOTES: _____

_____

_____

_____

THE LARGEST FISH IN THE SEA

Have you ever wondered: What's the largest fish in the sea? Well, you're not alone. The whale shark is the largest fish species on Earth. Contrary to its confusing name, it's a fish, not a mammal, but, like whales, it is huge: the largest known individual was more than 40 feet long. That's about the length of a semi-trailer. A filter feeder, the whale shark eats huge amounts of tiny plankton to sustain its size. The biggest fish of all time, though, was *Leedsichthys problematicus*. Alive around 160 million years ago, it was 50-plus-feet long, and it was fast, too, with a top speed of around 11 miles an hour.

SPECIES: _____ DATE: _____

LOCATION: _____

BAIT: _____

NOTES: _____

_____

_____

_____

SPECIES: _____ DATE: _____
LOCATION: _____
BAIT: _____
NOTES: _____
_____
_____
_____

SPECIES: _____ DATE: _____
LOCATION: _____
BAIT: _____
NOTES: _____
_____
_____
_____

SPECIES: _____ DATE: _____
LOCATION: _____
BAIT: _____
NOTES: _____
_____
_____
_____

SPECIES: _____ DATE: _____
LOCATION: _____
BAIT: _____
NOTES: _____
_____
_____
_____

SPECIES: _____ DATE: _____
LOCATION: _____
BAIT: _____
NOTES: _____
_____
_____
_____

SPECIES: _____ DATE: _____

LOCATION: _____

BAIT: _____

NOTES: _____

_____

_____

_____

SPECIES: _____ DATE: _____

LOCATION: _____

BAIT: _____

NOTES: _____

_____

_____

_____

SPECIES: _____ DATE: _____

LOCATION: _____

BAIT: _____

NOTES: _____

_____

_____

_____

SPECIES: _____ DATE: _____

LOCATION: _____

BAIT: _____

NOTES: _____

_____

_____

_____

SPECIES: _____ DATE: _____

LOCATION: _____

BAIT: _____

NOTES: _____

_____

_____

_____

SPECIES: DATE:

LOCATION:

BAIT:

NOTES:

SPECIES: DATE:

LOCATION:

BAIT:

NOTES:

SPECIES: DATE:

LOCATION:

BAIT:

NOTES:

SPECIES: DATE:

LOCATION:

BAIT:

NOTES:

SPECIES: DATE:

LOCATION:

BAIT:

NOTES:

SPECIES: _____   DATE: _____

LOCATION: _____

BAIT: _____

NOTES: _____

_____

_____

SPECIES: _____   DATE: _____

LOCATION: _____

BAIT: _____

NOTES: _____

_____

_____

SPECIES: _____   DATE: _____

LOCATION: _____

BAIT: _____

NOTES: _____

_____

_____

SPECIES: _____   DATE: _____

LOCATION: _____

BAIT: _____

NOTES: _____

_____

_____

SPECIES: _____   DATE: _____

LOCATION: _____

BAIT: _____

NOTES: _____

_____

_____

THE SMALLEST FISH ON EARTH, AND IN NORTH AMERICA

You may have caught some tiny fish in your time as an angler, but nothing like the least killifish. The smallest fish in North America is a relative of guppies and mollies, the aquarium standards. Adult males reach a maximum length of just under an inch, with adult females just over an inch. The world's smallest fish, *Paedocypris progenetica*, is even tinier. Hailing from Indonesia, adults of its species are under one-third of an inch in length.

SPECIES: DATE:

LOCATION:

BAIT:

NOTES:

SPECIES: DATE:

LOCATION:

BAIT:

NOTES:

THE FIRST FISHING HOOK

People have been fishing forever, but have you ever wondered just how long? Well, as it happens, archaeologists have an answer—for at least 42,000 years. Researchers at a site in East Timor found a cave site that was replete in fish bones—including many deep-sea species—as well as fish hooks fashioned out of shell fragments that were produced later. These finds aren't unique: similarly old fish hooks have been found in Papua New Guinea and elsewhere. The first fish hooks from North America date back to 11,000 years, though evidence of human habitation of the Americas is a lot older than that, with one site in Chile dating back to at least 16,500 years ago. And if that's not enough fishing trivia for you, the theory that the first peoples arrived in the Americas by traveling on a land bridge across the Bering Strait has fallen out of favor. Now, the general consensus is that people arrived by a route along the coast—probably by boat.

SPECIES: _____ DATE: _____

LOCATION: _____

BAIT: _____

NOTES: _____

_____

_____

SPECIES: _____ DATE: _____

LOCATION: _____

BAIT: _____

NOTES: _____

_____

_____

SPECIES: _____ DATE: _____

LOCATION: _____

BAIT: _____

NOTES: _____

_____

_____

SPECIES: _____ DATE: _____

LOCATION: _____

BAIT: _____

NOTES: _____

_____

_____

SPECIES: _____ DATE: _____

LOCATION: _____

BAIT: _____

NOTES: _____

_____

_____

SPECIES: DATE:

LOCATION:

BAIT:

NOTES:

SPECIES: DATE:

LOCATION:

BAIT:

NOTES:

SPECIES: DATE:

LOCATION:

BAIT:

NOTES:

SPECIES: DATE:

LOCATION:

BAIT:

NOTES:

SPECIES: DATE:

LOCATION:

BAIT:

NOTES:

SPECIES: _____ DATE: _____

LOCATION: _____

BAIT: _____

NOTES: _____

_____

_____

_____

SPECIES: _____ DATE: _____

LOCATION: _____

BAIT: _____

NOTES: _____

_____

_____

_____

SPECIES: _____ DATE: _____

LOCATION: _____

BAIT: _____

NOTES: _____

_____

_____

_____

SPECIES: _____ DATE: _____

LOCATION: _____

BAIT: _____

NOTES: _____

_____

_____

_____

SPECIES: _____ DATE: _____

LOCATION: _____

BAIT: _____

NOTES: _____

_____

_____

_____

SPECIES: _____ DATE: _____

LOCATION: _____

BAIT: _____

NOTES: _____

_____

_____

_____

SPECIES: _____ DATE: _____

LOCATION: _____

BAIT: _____

NOTES: _____

_____

_____

_____

SPECIES: _____ DATE: _____

LOCATION: _____

BAIT: _____

NOTES: _____

_____

_____

_____

SPECIES: _____ DATE: _____

LOCATION: _____

BAIT: _____

NOTES: _____

_____

_____

_____

SPECIES: _____ DATE: _____

LOCATION: _____

BAIT: _____

NOTES: _____

_____

_____

_____

GOING PRO

It's a dream job: getting paid to fish. But for a select few—professional anglers—it's a reality, and for elite anglers of highly sought-after species such as bass, there's real money to be made. According to B.A.S.S., the group that runs the famous Bassmaster tournaments, nearly 50 anglers have earned more than $1 million over the course of their tournament careers. The top earner has amassed more than $4 million in winnings. While professional bass fishing is lucrative, fishing for marlin in the Bisbee's Black and Blue tournament can offer even more money: in 2018, an angling team won more than $3 million.

SPECIES: _____   DATE: _____

LOCATION: _____

BAIT: _____

NOTES: _____

_____

_____

_____

FOR GREAT DELIGHT IT IS FOR EYE AND MIND TO SEE THE CAPTIVE FISH TOSSING AND TURNING.

– the Halieutica, by Oppian, among the first works dedicated solely to fishing, circa 200 BCE

SPECIES: _____ DATE: _____

LOCATION: _____

BAIT: _____

NOTES: _____

_____

_____

SPECIES: _____ DATE: _____

LOCATION: _____

BAIT: _____

NOTES: _____

_____

_____

SPECIES: _____ DATE: _____

LOCATION: _____

BAIT: _____

NOTES: _____

_____

_____

SPECIES: _____ DATE: _____

LOCATION: _____

BAIT: _____

NOTES: _____

_____

_____

SPECIES: DATE:

LOCATION:

BAIT:

NOTES:

SPECIES: DATE:

LOCATION:

BAIT:

NOTES:

SPECIES: DATE:

LOCATION:

BAIT:

NOTES:

SPECIES: DATE:

LOCATION:

BAIT:

NOTES:

SPECIES: DATE:

LOCATION:

BAIT:

NOTES:

SPECIES: _____ DATE: _____

LOCATION: _____

BAIT: _____

NOTES: _____

_____

_____

_____

SPECIES: _____ DATE: _____

LOCATION: _____

BAIT: _____

NOTES: _____

_____

_____

_____

SPECIES: _____ DATE: _____

LOCATION: _____

BAIT: _____

NOTES: _____

_____

_____

_____

SPECIES: _____ DATE: _____

LOCATION: _____

BAIT: _____

NOTES: _____

_____

_____

_____

SPECIES: _____ DATE: _____

LOCATION: _____

BAIT: _____

NOTES: _____

_____

_____

_____

ALL ABOUT FISHING LINE

The first fishing lines consisted of natural substances, such as hair, silk, or material found in the intestines of domestic animals, which is known as catgut. (Despite the name, cats weren't the source of the material; it was usually sheep or goats.) Once the industrial revolution arrived, factories produced fishing line made out of cotton and other fibers. As odd as it seems today, monofilament lines are a relatively recent invention, as they were first released for sale in the middle part of the twentieth century. That might seem surprising, given how ubiquitous such line is now and the sometimes-bewildering number of products currently on the market.

SPECIES: _____ DATE: _____

LOCATION: _____

BAIT: _____

NOTES: _____

_____

_____

_____

SPECIES: _____ DATE: _____

LOCATION: _____

BAIT: _____

NOTES: _____

_____

_____

_____

SPECIES: _____ DATE: _____

LOCATION: _____

BAIT: _____

NOTES: _____

_____

_____

_____

SPECIES: _____ DATE: _____

LOCATION: _____

BAIT: _____

NOTES: _____

_____

_____

_____

SPECIES: _____ DATE: _____

LOCATION: _____

BAIT: _____

NOTES: _____

_____

_____

_____

SPECIES: _____ DATE: _____

LOCATION: _____

BAIT: _____

NOTES: _____

_____

_____

_____

SPECIES: _____ DATE: _____

LOCATION: _____

BAIT: _____

NOTES: _____

_____

_____

_____

SPECIES: _____ DATE: _____

LOCATION: _____

BAIT: _____

NOTES: _____

_____

_____

_____

SPECIES: _____ DATE: _____

LOCATION: _____

BAIT: _____

NOTES: _____

_____

_____

_____

SPECIES: _____ DATE: _____

LOCATION: _____

BAIT: _____

NOTES: _____

_____

_____

_____

INVASIVE FISH: SEA LAMPREY

The fisheries of the Great Lakes have changed a great deal over the past century in large part due to the accidental introduction of an invasive species: the sea lamprey. Resembling an eel, but with a nightmare of a mouth, the sea lamprey spread from Lake Ontario to the rest of the Great Lakes via the Welland Canal around 1919. It then decimated the resident fish populations. (To feed, the lampreys simply "hook on" to the outside of a fish with their rasping mouths and then drink out the liquified fish parts.) They had a terrible impact on lake trout, ciscoes, and whitefish—the backbone of the Great Lakes fisheries. The good news is that scientists have established ways to reduce sea lamprey populations dramatically, and now efforts are underway to help native fish populations recover.

SPECIES: _____ DATE: _____

LOCATION: _____

BAIT: _____

NOTES: _____

_____

_____

_____

SPECIES: _____ DATE: _____

LOCATION: _____

BAIT: _____

NOTES: _____

_____

_____

_____

SPECIES: _____ DATE: _____

LOCATION: _____

BAIT: _____

NOTES: _____

_____

_____

_____

SPECIES: _____ DATE: _____

LOCATION: _____

BAIT: _____

NOTES: _____

_____

_____

_____

SPECIES: _____ DATE: _____

LOCATION: _____

BAIT: _____

NOTES: _____

_____

_____

_____

SPECIES: _____ DATE: _____

LOCATION: _____

BAIT: _____

NOTES: _____

_____

_____

_____

SPECIES: _____ DATE: _____

LOCATION: _____

BAIT: _____

NOTES: _____

_____

_____

SPECIES: _____ DATE: _____

LOCATION: _____

BAIT: _____

NOTES: _____

_____

_____

SPECIES: _____ DATE: _____

LOCATION: _____

BAIT: _____

NOTES: _____

_____

_____

SPECIES: _____ DATE: _____

LOCATION: _____

BAIT: _____

NOTES: _____

_____

_____

SPECIES: _____ DATE: _____

LOCATION: _____

BAIT: _____

NOTES: _____

_____

_____

_____

SPECIES: _____ DATE: _____

LOCATION: _____

BAIT: _____

NOTES: _____

_____

_____

_____

SPECIES: _____ DATE: _____

LOCATION: _____

BAIT: _____

NOTES: _____

_____

_____

_____

SPECIES: _____ DATE: _____

LOCATION: _____

BAIT: _____

NOTES: _____

_____

_____

_____

SPECIES: _____ DATE: _____

LOCATION: _____

BAIT: _____

NOTES: _____

_____

_____

_____

SPECIES: _____ DATE: _____

LOCATION: _____

BAIT: _____

NOTES: _____

_____

_____

_____

SPECIES: _____ DATE: _____

LOCATION: _____

BAIT: _____

NOTES: _____

_____

_____

_____

SPECIES: _____ DATE: _____

LOCATION: _____

BAIT: _____

NOTES: _____

_____

_____

_____

SPECIES: _____ DATE: _____

LOCATION: _____

BAIT: _____

NOTES: _____

_____

_____

_____

SPECIES: _____ DATE: _____

LOCATION: _____

BAIT: _____

NOTES: _____

_____

_____

_____

SPECIES: _____ DATE: _____

LOCATION: _____

BAIT: _____

NOTES: _____

_____

_____

_____

INVASIVE FISH: ASIAN CARP

Carp belong to a fish family that has been widely introduced around the world. Carp were among the first fish that were farmed, with carp aquaculture dating back thousands of years. The common carp, a European native, was introduced to the U.S. in the nineteenth century and is now found in nearly every state, and it is often among the most common fish in some bodies of water. More recently, several varieties of Asian carp have been introduced into the U.S. that threaten our waters. In particular, the silver carp, the bighead carp, and the grass carp are all present in—or a threat to—the Upper Mississippi River and the Great Lakes. The silver carp, in particular, is perhaps the most well-known threat, thanks to its size (60 pounds or more) and its tremendous leaps out of the water—up to 10 feet—when startled. This makes it a real threat to boaters and those enjoying time on the water, and serious injuries (including broken bones) have been reported. And once it's established in an area, this fish likes to stay: like its cousins, the silver carp reproduces incredibly quickly (a single female can produce more than 2 million eggs).

SPECIES: _____ DATE: _____

LOCATION: _____

BAIT: _____

NOTES: _____

_____

_____

_____

SPECIES: _____ DATE: _____

LOCATION: _____

BAIT: _____

NOTES: _____

_____

_____

_____

SPECIES: _____ DATE: _____

LOCATION: _____

BAIT: _____

NOTES: _____

_____

_____

_____

SPECIES: _____ DATE: _____

LOCATION: _____

BAIT: _____

NOTES: _____

_____

_____

_____

SPECIES: _____ DATE: _____

LOCATION: _____

BAIT: _____

NOTES: _____

_____

_____

_____

SPECIES: _____ DATE: _____

LOCATION: _____

BAIT: _____

NOTES: _____

_____

_____

_____

SPECIES: _____ DATE: _____

LOCATION: _____

BAIT: _____

NOTES: _____

_____

_____

_____

SPECIES: _____ DATE: _____

LOCATION: _____

BAIT: _____

NOTES: _____

_____

_____

_____

SPECIES: _____ DATE: _____

LOCATION: _____

BAIT: _____

NOTES: _____

_____

_____

_____

SPECIES: _____ DATE: _____

LOCATION: _____

BAIT: _____

NOTES: _____

_____

_____

_____

INVASIVE FISH: FRANKENFISH
(NORTHERN SNAKEHEADS)

A popular food fish in its native Asia, the northern snakehead is one of the more troubling invasive species introduced to the United States in recent years. Originally sold as an aquarium denizen and as a food fish, released snakeheads were discovered in a Maryland pond. Their voracious appetite and blinding speed, coupled with their uncanny ability to survive by breathing air when necessary, has made them a serious threat. Populations are now established in sections of the Potomac River and may be in Florida and other areas. The initial discovery of the northern snakeheads quickly led to a nickname—Frankenfish—and soon thereafter, not one, but three, horror movies based on the events were released.

SPECIES: _____ DATE: _____

LOCATION: _____

BAIT: _____

NOTES: _____

_____

_____

_____

SPECIES: _____ DATE: _____

LOCATION: _____

BAIT: _____

NOTES: _____

_____

_____

_____

SPECIES: _____ DATE: _____

LOCATION: _____

BAIT: _____

NOTES: _____

_____

_____

_____

SPECIES: _____ DATE: _____

LOCATION: _____

BAIT: _____

NOTES: _____

_____

_____

_____

SPECIES: _____ DATE: _____

LOCATION: _____

BAIT: _____

NOTES: _____

_____

_____

_____

SPECIES: _____ DATE: _____

LOCATION: _____

BAIT: _____

NOTES: _____

_____

_____

_____

SPECIES: _____ DATE: _____

LOCATION: _____

BAIT: _____

NOTES: _____

_____

_____

_____

SPECIES: _____ DATE: _____

LOCATION: _____

BAIT: _____

NOTES: _____

_____

_____

_____

SPECIES: _____ DATE: _____

LOCATION: _____

BAIT: _____

NOTES: _____

_____

_____

_____

SPECIES: _____ DATE: _____

LOCATION: _____

BAIT: _____

NOTES: _____

_____

_____

_____

SPECIES: _____ DATE: _____

LOCATION: _____

BAIT: _____

NOTES: _____

_____

_____

_____

SPECIES: _____ DATE: _____

LOCATION: _____

BAIT: _____

NOTES: _____

_____

_____

_____

SPECIES: _____ DATE: _____

LOCATION: _____

BAIT: _____

NOTES: _____

_____

_____

_____

SPECIES: _____ DATE: _____

LOCATION: _____

BAIT: _____

NOTES: _____

_____

_____

_____

SPECIES: _____ DATE: _____

LOCATION: _____

BAIT: _____

NOTES: _____

_____

_____

_____

SPECIES: _____ DATE: _____

LOCATION: _____

BAIT: _____

NOTES: _____

_____

_____

_____

SPECIES: _____ DATE: _____

LOCATION: _____

BAIT: _____

NOTES: _____

_____

_____

_____

SPECIES: _____ DATE: _____

LOCATION: _____

BAIT: _____

NOTES: _____

_____

_____

_____

SPECIES: _____ DATE: _____

LOCATION: _____

BAIT: _____

NOTES: _____

_____

_____

_____

SPECIES: _____ DATE: _____

LOCATION: _____

BAIT: _____

NOTES: _____

_____

_____

_____

BULLHEAD

ROUGH FISH

Not every fish variety is sought after. Some fish are ignored, actively avoided, or detested altogether. Often labeled "rough fish," these fish are not popular with most anglers. Common freshwater examples include bullheads, bowfin, eelpout, carp, suckers, and redhorses. But for some anglers, rough fish are their own sort of prize. Often relatively abundant, large, and subjected to markedly less fishing pressure, rough fish are often a surefire way to find fishing excitement. Some can even be excellent table fare.

SPECIES: DATE:

LOCATION:

BAIT:

NOTES:

SPECIES: _____ DATE: _____

LOCATION: _____

BAIT: _____

NOTES: _____

_____

_____

_____

SPECIES: _____ DATE: _____

LOCATION: _____

BAIT: _____

NOTES: _____

_____

_____

_____

SPECIES: _____ DATE: _____

LOCATION: _____

BAIT: _____

NOTES: _____

_____

_____

_____

SPECIES: _____ DATE: _____

LOCATION: _____

BAIT: _____

NOTES: _____

_____

_____

_____

SPECIES: _____ DATE: _____

LOCATION: _____

BAIT: _____

NOTES: _____

_____

_____

_____

SPECIES: _____ DATE: _____

LOCATION: _____

BAIT: _____

NOTES: _____

_____

_____

_____

SPECIES: _____ DATE: _____

LOCATION: _____

BAIT: _____

NOTES: _____

_____

_____

_____

SPECIES: _____ DATE: _____

LOCATION: _____

BAIT: _____

NOTES: _____

_____

_____

_____

SPECIES: _____ DATE: _____

LOCATION: _____

BAIT: _____

NOTES: _____

_____

_____

_____

SPECIES: _____ DATE: _____

LOCATION: _____

BAIT: _____

NOTES: _____

_____

_____

_____

SPECIES: DATE:

LOCATION:

BAIT:

NOTES:

SPECIES: DATE:

LOCATION:

BAIT:

NOTES:

SPECIES: DATE:

LOCATION:

BAIT:

NOTES:

SPECIES: DATE:

LOCATION:

BAIT:

NOTES:

SPECIES: DATE:

LOCATION:

BAIT:

NOTES:

NOODLING

You don't necessarily need a rod and a reel to catch a fish. Or even a net. Some adventurous folks, largely in the southern part of the country, catch catfish with just their hands. Known as "noodling," the process is pretty simple, albeit potentially dangerous. When catfish spawn, the female lays eggs amid an underwater structure, often a hole that the catfish digs itself. Once a catfish hole is located, the noodler places a hand inside, and the catfish latches onto it. The catfish, which can often weigh upwards of 40 pounds, is then lifted out of the water. Noodling can be a dangerous pastime, however. Catfish holes are often home to other animals, including snakes, alligators, and beavers. Injuries, and sometimes deaths (often by drowning), have occurred. It's probably best to leave this pastime to the experts.

FLATHEAD CATFISH

SPECIES: _____ DATE: _____

LOCATION: _____

BAIT: _____

NOTES: _____

_____

_____

_____

SPECIES: _____ DATE: _____

LOCATION: _____

BAIT: _____

NOTES: _____

_____

_____

_____

SPECIES: _____ DATE: _____

LOCATION: _____

BAIT: _____

NOTES: _____

_____

_____

_____

SPECIES: _____ DATE: _____

LOCATION: _____

BAIT: _____

NOTES: _____

_____

_____

_____

SPECIES: _____ DATE: _____

LOCATION: _____

BAIT: _____

NOTES: _____

_____

_____

_____

SPECIES: _____ DATE: _____

LOCATION: _____

BAIT: _____

NOTES: _____

_____

_____

_____

SPECIES: _____ DATE: _____

LOCATION: _____

BAIT: _____

NOTES: _____

_____

_____

_____

SPECIES: _____ DATE: _____

LOCATION: _____

BAIT: _____

NOTES: _____

_____

_____

_____

SPECIES: _____ DATE: _____

LOCATION: _____

BAIT: _____

NOTES: _____

_____

_____

_____

SPECIES: _____ DATE: _____

LOCATION: _____

BAIT: _____

NOTES: _____

_____

_____

_____

THE STATES WITH THE MOST ANGLERS

According to the U.S. Fish and Wildlife Service, more than 30 million Americans have recently held a fishing license. But some states have more licensed anglers than others. In a recent year, Texas (pop. 28.7 million), California (pop. 39.5 million), and Florida (pop. 21.3 million) rounded out the top of the list, with 1,900,000, 1,635,000, and 1,547,000 paid license holders, respectively. But Minnesota, which is relatively tiny in comparison, comes in fourth. With a population of just 5.6 million, it boasts 1,448,000 holders of a fishing license, with approximately 1,288,000 of them residents. That means that approximately 20 percent of the entire state's population has a fishing license. (And that doesn't count the resident kiddos under 16, who don't need a license in Minnesota.) Similar license-to-population ratios can be found in plenty of other relatively small, but fishing-crazed, states, including Wisconsin, Michigan, and Idaho.

SPECIES: _____   DATE: _____

LOCATION: _____

BAIT: _____

NOTES: _____

_____

_____

_____

SPECIES: _____ DATE: _____

LOCATION: _____

BAIT: _____

NOTES: _____

_____

_____

SPECIES: _____ DATE: _____

LOCATION: _____

BAIT: _____

NOTES: _____

_____

_____

SPECIES: _____ DATE: _____

LOCATION: _____

BAIT: _____

NOTES: _____

_____

_____

SPECIES: _____ DATE: _____

LOCATION: _____

BAIT: _____

NOTES: _____

_____

_____

SPECIES: _____ DATE: _____

LOCATION: _____

BAIT: _____

NOTES: _____

_____

_____

SPECIES: _____ DATE: _____

LOCATION: _____

BAIT: _____

NOTES: _____

_____

_____

_____

SPECIES: _____ DATE: _____

LOCATION: _____

BAIT: _____

NOTES: _____

_____

_____

_____

SPECIES: _____ DATE: _____

LOCATION: _____

BAIT: _____

NOTES: _____

_____

_____

_____

SPECIES: _____ DATE: _____

LOCATION: _____

BAIT: _____

NOTES: _____

_____

_____

_____

SPECIES: _____ DATE: _____

LOCATION: _____

BAIT: _____

NOTES: _____

_____

_____

_____

SPECIES: _____   DATE: _____

LOCATION: _____

BAIT: _____

NOTES: _____

_____

_____

_____

SPECIES: _____   DATE: _____

LOCATION: _____

BAIT: _____

NOTES: _____

_____

_____

_____

FAMOUS FISH

Every body of water seemingly has a lunker that everyone talks about, whether it's a record muskie spotted, but not caught, in the North Woods of Minnesota, or a big bass lost just at the boat. Sometimes, such fish even get their own names and a devoted following. That's what happened in Britain in the case of "The Parrot," a beloved carp that was an amazing 68 pounds, 1 ounce, and the freshwater record there. A reliable striker, caught again and again, it was a favorite of anglers, who all wanted a chance to heft it up for a photo. According to *The Independent*, it died of natural causes in 2016, leading anglers the world over to memorialize it—some were reputedly even in tears at a memorial service held for the fish, which was informally known as a "marriage wrecker."

SPECIES: _____ DATE: _____

LOCATION: _____

BAIT: _____

NOTES: _____

_____

_____

_____

SPECIES: _____ DATE: _____

LOCATION: _____

BAIT: _____

NOTES: _____

_____

_____

_____

SPECIES: _____ DATE: _____

LOCATION: _____

BAIT: _____

NOTES: _____

_____

_____

_____

SPECIES: _____ DATE: _____

LOCATION: _____

BAIT: _____

NOTES: _____

_____

_____

_____

SPECIES: _____ DATE: _____

LOCATION: _____

BAIT: _____

NOTES: _____

_____

_____

_____

SPECIES: _____ DATE: _____

LOCATION: _____

BAIT: _____

NOTES: _____

_____

_____

_____

SPECIES: _____ DATE: _____

LOCATION: _____

BAIT: _____

NOTES: _____

_____

_____

_____

SPECIES: _____ DATE: _____

LOCATION: _____

BAIT: _____

NOTES: _____

_____

_____

_____

SPECIES: _____ DATE: _____

LOCATION: _____

BAIT: _____

NOTES: _____

_____

_____

_____

HIS TAIL I GRASP WITH EAGER HAND, AND SWING, WITH JOY, MY PRIZE ON LAND.

– The Angler's Songbook (1855)

NINESPINE STICKLEBACK

MICROFISHING

Most anglers try to catch big fish, but that's not always true. Some folks are after tiny fish. In a hobby known as microfishing, these fans of tiny fish are out to find, and catch, fish that most anglers might not even know about. Similar to how birders keep "life lists" of species observed, these "microfishers" seek out as many species as possible. And there are plenty of fish to find; approximately 1,200 fish species are in the U.S.

Of course, catching tiny fish takes, well, tiny gear. When microfishing, anglers often have to create their own gear and strategies, sometimes even hand-lining to catch fish. While it's obviously still a relatively tiny (no pun intended) subset of anglers, those who get into it are absolutely enthralled by it and become devotees.

SPECIES: DATE:

LOCATION:

BAIT:

NOTES:

SPECIES: DATE:

LOCATION:

BAIT:

NOTES:

SPECIES: DATE:

LOCATION:

BAIT:

NOTES:

SPECIES: DATE:

LOCATION:

BAIT:

NOTES:

SPECIES: DATE:

LOCATION:

BAIT:

NOTES:

SPECIES: _____ DATE: _____

LOCATION: _____

BAIT: _____

NOTES: _____

_____

_____

_____

SPECIES: _____ DATE: _____

LOCATION: _____

BAIT: _____

NOTES: _____

_____

_____

_____

SPECIES: _____ DATE: _____

LOCATION: _____

BAIT: _____

NOTES: _____

_____

_____

_____

SPECIES: _____ DATE: _____

LOCATION: _____

BAIT: _____

NOTES: _____

_____

_____

_____

SPECIES: _____ DATE: _____

LOCATION: _____

BAIT: _____

NOTES: _____

_____

_____

_____

SPECIES: _____ DATE: _____

LOCATION: _____

BAIT: _____

NOTES: _____

_____

_____

_____

SPECIES: _____ DATE: _____

LOCATION: _____

BAIT: _____

NOTES: _____

_____

_____

_____

SPECIES: _____ DATE: _____

LOCATION: _____

BAIT: _____

NOTES: _____

_____

_____

_____

SPECIES: _____ DATE: _____

LOCATION: _____

BAIT: _____

NOTES: _____

_____

_____

_____

SPECIES: _____ DATE: _____

LOCATION: _____

BAIT: _____

NOTES: _____

_____

_____

_____

SPECIES: DATE:

LOCATION:

BAIT:

NOTES:

___

SPECIES: DATE:

LOCATION:

BAIT:

NOTES:

___

SPECIES: DATE:

LOCATION:

BAIT:

NOTES:

___

SPECIES: DATE:

LOCATION:

BAIT:

NOTES:

___

SPECIES: DATE:

LOCATION:

BAIT:

NOTES:

EATING THE INVASIVES

When invasive species become entrenched in a habitat, there often aren't many good options. Chemical control of invasives is difficult and often affects native species. And invasive species, by definition, lack natural predators to keep them in check, so once they're established, it's often for good. Nonetheless, there are ways to fight back. The simplest is an old-fashioned bounty. In the Pacific Northwest, northern pike have been introduced in a number of bodies of water, and the aggressive predators have wreaked havoc. To combat them, a number of organizations have offered bounties—often $10 or $20 per fish. (In areas where the pike is beloved, this has no doubt led many anglers to consider quitting their jobs and head out west.)

In other areas, say, with Asian carp or sea lampreys in the Midwest, there's a more straightforward method of control: eating 'em! Invasives are often (somewhat unfairly) maligned as poor table fare, often because they're simply unfamiliar to residents. Campaigns to endear them to anglers' palates have sometimes involved local chefs and specialized recipes, and even business plans that commercially harvest the invasive critter and sell it to countries abroad where it's a staple, or in the case of lampreys in parts of Europe, a delicacy. (Speaking of lampreys, King Henry I of England was reputed to have died from a "surfeit of lampreys" way back in 1135.)

SEA LAMPREY

SPECIES: _____ DATE: _____

LOCATION: _____

BAIT: _____

NOTES: _____

_____

_____

_____

SPECIES: _____ DATE: _____

LOCATION: _____

BAIT: _____

NOTES: _____

_____

_____

_____

SPECIES: _____ DATE: _____

LOCATION: _____

BAIT: _____

NOTES: _____

_____

_____

_____

SPECIES: _____ DATE: _____

LOCATION: _____

BAIT: _____

NOTES: _____

_____

_____

_____

SPECIES: _____ DATE: _____

LOCATION: _____

BAIT: _____

NOTES: _____

_____

_____

_____

SPECIES: DATE:

LOCATION:

BAIT:

NOTES:

SPECIES: DATE:

LOCATION:

BAIT:

NOTES:

SPECIES: DATE:

LOCATION:

BAIT:

NOTES:

SPECIES: DATE:

LOCATION:

BAIT:

NOTES:

SPECIES: DATE:

LOCATION:

BAIT:

NOTES:

A NEW STYLE OF TAXIDERMY

When you catch a really big fish, you're faced with a choice: Do you put it back, so others can catch it? Or do you have a taxidermied mount of the fish created, which will kill it? Happily, with the advent of modern technology, there's now another option. Digital cameras have advanced to the point where companies now offer lifelike fish reproductions based on your photographs. Such mounts are works of art, and they offer the best of both worlds—a way for anglers to memorialize their trophies while preserving the resource. (Plus, such mounts have another advantage over traditional taxidermy—they don't require eventual maintenance like taxidermied mounts do.)

SPECIES: _____ DATE: _____

LOCATION: _____

BAIT: _____

NOTES: _____

_____

_____

_____

SPECIES: _____ DATE: _____

LOCATION: _____

BAIT: _____

NOTES: _____

_____

_____

_____

SPECIES: _____ DATE: _____

LOCATION: _____

BAIT: _____

NOTES: _____

_____

_____

_____

SPECIES: _____ DATE: _____

LOCATION: _____

BAIT: _____

NOTES: _____

_____

_____

_____

SPECIES: _____ DATE: _____

LOCATION: _____

BAIT: _____

NOTES: _____

_____

_____

_____

SPECIES: _____ DATE: _____

LOCATION: _____

BAIT: _____

NOTES: _____

_____

_____

_____

SPECIES: _____ DATE: _____

LOCATION: _____

BAIT: _____

NOTES: _____

_____

_____

_____

SPECIES: _____ DATE: _____

LOCATION: _____

BAIT: _____

NOTES: _____

_____

_____

_____

SPECIES: _____ DATE: _____

LOCATION: _____

BAIT: _____

NOTES: _____

_____

_____

_____

SPECIES: _____ DATE: _____

LOCATION: _____

BAIT: _____

NOTES: _____

_____

_____

_____

SPECIES: DATE:

LOCATION:

BAIT:

NOTES:

SPECIES: DATE:

LOCATION:

BAIT:

NOTES:

SPECIES: DATE:

LOCATION:

BAIT:

NOTES:

SPECIES: DATE:

LOCATION:

BAIT:

NOTES:

SPECIES: DATE:

LOCATION:

BAIT:

NOTES:

SPECIES: DATE:

LOCATION:

BAIT:

NOTES:

___

SPECIES: DATE:

LOCATION:

BAIT:

NOTES:

___

SPECIES: DATE:

LOCATION:

BAIT:

NOTES:

___

SPECIES: DATE:

LOCATION:

BAIT:

NOTES:

___

SPECIES: DATE:

LOCATION:

BAIT:

NOTES:

BIGGER BOATS (AND ENGINES)

You don't need a big boat, or a big engine, to catch fish. You can catch fish just by casting when you're out on a paddleboat or drifting along in a kayak. But a modern boat, with a modern engine, sure doesn't hurt. It's amazing to think about how much has changed in terms of boat design over the past few decades. Not long ago, it wasn't uncommon to see boats with 25-horsepower engines, or even smaller. Today, 200-horsepower engines aren't uncommon, and boats outfitted with the latest technology can run into tens of thousands of dollars. Fishing—and boats in general—have always had a well-deserved reputation for being expensive—the old joke that getting a boat is like setting your money on fire is still true—but today the potential fire is bigger than ever.

SPECIES: _____ DATE: _____

LOCATION: _____

BAIT: _____

NOTES: _____

_____

_____

_____

SPECIES: _____ DATE: _____

LOCATION: _____

BAIT: _____

NOTES: _____

_____

_____

_____

SPECIES: _____ DATE: _____

LOCATION: _____

BAIT: _____

NOTES: _____

_____

_____

_____

SPECIES: _____ DATE: _____

LOCATION: _____

BAIT: _____

NOTES: _____

_____

_____

_____

SPECIES: _____ DATE: _____

LOCATION: _____

BAIT: _____

NOTES: _____

_____

_____

_____

SPECIES: _____ DATE: _____

LOCATION: _____

BAIT: _____

NOTES: _____

_____

_____

_____

SPECIES: _____ DATE: _____

LOCATION: _____

BAIT: _____

NOTES: _____

_____

_____

_____

SPECIES: _____ DATE: _____

LOCATION: _____

BAIT: _____

NOTES: _____

_____

_____

_____

SPECIES: _____ DATE: _____

LOCATION: _____

BAIT: _____

NOTES: _____

_____

_____

_____

SPECIES: _____ DATE: _____

LOCATION: _____

BAIT: _____

NOTES: _____

_____

_____

_____

SPECIES: _____ DATE: _____

LOCATION: _____

BAIT: _____

NOTES: _____

_____

_____

_____

CASTABLE CAMERAS, GPS-ENABLED DEPTH FINDERS, AND MORE

For most of its history, fishing was, in theory, a relatively simple pastime: all you really needed was a hook, a rod, and a line. That's still true today, but for the technology inclined, there's more high-tech fishing gear available now than ever before. The list of gizmos gets longer each year: fish cameras, which were once primitive, black-and-white gadgets you had to peer into, are full-color, and relatively affordable. Depth finders, which once resembled something like a Speak-and-Spell, are now GPS-enabled, can have touchscreens, and are outfitted with sensors once only found on military vessels. All of this technological largesse costs money, of course, and while fishing has always been a good way to empty the ol' bank account, perhaps that's true today more than ever before.

SPECIES: _____   DATE: _____

LOCATION: _____

BAIT: _____

NOTES: _____

_____

_____

_____

SPECIES: DATE:

LOCATION:

BAIT:

NOTES:

SPECIES: DATE:

LOCATION:

BAIT:

NOTES:

SPECIES: DATE:

LOCATION:

BAIT:

NOTES:

SPECIES: DATE:

LOCATION:

BAIT:

NOTES:

SPECIES: DATE:

LOCATION:

BAIT:

NOTES:

SPECIES: _____   DATE: _____

LOCATION: _____

BAIT: _____

NOTES: _____

_____

_____

_____

SPECIES: _____   DATE: _____

LOCATION: _____

BAIT: _____

NOTES: _____

_____

_____

_____

SPECIES: _____   DATE: _____

LOCATION: _____

BAIT: _____

NOTES: _____

_____

_____

_____

SPECIES: _____   DATE: _____

LOCATION: _____

BAIT: _____

NOTES: _____

_____

_____

_____

SPECIES: _____   DATE: _____

LOCATION: _____

BAIT: _____

NOTES: _____

_____

_____

_____

SPECIES: _____   DATE: _____

LOCATION: _____

BAIT: _____

NOTES: _____

_____

_____

SPECIES: _____   DATE: _____

LOCATION: _____

BAIT: _____

NOTES: _____

_____

_____

SPECIES: _____   DATE: _____

LOCATION: _____

BAIT: _____

NOTES: _____

_____

_____

SPECIES: _____   DATE: _____

LOCATION: _____

BAIT: _____

NOTES: _____

_____

_____

SPECIES: _____   DATE: _____

LOCATION: _____

BAIT: _____

NOTES: _____

_____

_____

LIONFISH: A MARINE INVASIVE

Lionfish are a marine fish native to the Indian and Pacific Oceans, but thanks to introductions (probably from aquarium specimens that got too big to keep), they're now established in large parts of the Gulf of Mexico, along the Southeast coast, and the Caribbean. Famous for their beautiful, long spines, they're also highly venomous—a sting from a lionfish can cause serious pain for an extended amount of time in a healthy individual and can prove deadly to children, the elderly, or those who are allergic to lionfish venom. The good news is that lionfish, when properly prepared, are tasty, and spearing them is one way to keep their populations in check. Lionfish fillets are now available—sometimes even at grocery stores—in parts of their invasive range. If you think you've never seen a lionfish, think again. On *Star Trek: The Next Generation*, a lionfish was Captain Picard's pet fish. Its name? Livingston.

SPECIES: _____ DATE: _____

LOCATION: _____

BAIT: _____

NOTES: _____

_____

_____

_____

SPECIES: _____ DATE: _____

LOCATION: _____

BAIT: _____

NOTES: _____

_____

_____

_____

SPECIES: _____ DATE: _____

LOCATION: _____

BAIT: _____

NOTES: _____

_____

_____

_____

SPECIES: _____ DATE: _____

LOCATION: _____

BAIT: _____

NOTES: _____

_____

_____

_____

SPECIES: _____ DATE: _____

LOCATION: _____

BAIT: _____

NOTES: _____

_____

_____

_____

SPECIES: _____ DATE: _____

LOCATION: _____

BAIT: _____

NOTES: _____

_____

_____

_____

SPECIES: _____ DATE: _____

LOCATION: _____

BAIT: _____

NOTES: _____

_____

_____

_____

SPECIES: _____ DATE: _____

LOCATION: _____

BAIT: _____

NOTES: _____

_____

_____

_____

SPECIES: _____ DATE: _____

LOCATION: _____

BAIT: _____

NOTES: _____

_____

_____

_____

SPECIES: _____ DATE: _____

LOCATION: _____

BAIT: _____

NOTES: _____

_____

_____

_____

SPECIES: _____ DATE: _____

LOCATION: _____

BAIT: _____

NOTES: _____

_____

_____

SPECIES: _____ DATE: _____

LOCATION: _____

BAIT: _____

NOTES: _____

_____

_____

SPECIES: _____ DATE: _____

LOCATION: _____

BAIT: _____

NOTES: _____

_____

_____

SPECIES: _____ DATE: _____

LOCATION: _____

BAIT: _____

NOTES: _____

_____

_____

SPECIES: _____ DATE: _____

LOCATION: _____

BAIT: _____

NOTES: _____

_____

_____

SPECIES: DATE:

LOCATION:

BAIT:

NOTES:

SPECIES: DATE:

LOCATION:

BAIT:

NOTES:

SPECIES: DATE:

LOCATION:

BAIT:

NOTES:

SPECIES: DATE:

LOCATION:

BAIT:

NOTES:

SPECIES: DATE:

LOCATION:

BAIT:

NOTES:

THE DEPTHS OF THE SEA

The Challenger Deep is the deepest-known portion of the world's oceans. Located in the Mariana Trench in the Pacific Ocean, it is 35,755 feet deep. It has been visited by humans only on a handful of occasions—more people have walked on the moon. The first visit occurred in the bathysphere *Trieste* in 1960 by Jacques Piccard and Don Walsh, and manned follow-up visits occurred only much later, in 2012 when director James Cameron visited, and in 2019, when Victor Vescovo arrived. One of the outstanding questions of all these visits is simple: What is life like at the bottom? The crew of the *Trieste* reported seeing fish, just above the maximum depth, but Cameron and Vescovo found no evidence of fish on their visit, and it's been since postulated that no fish may exist below a certain depth because of the effects of the incredible water pressure. But there's certainly life: All parties report seeing isopods (shrimp-like creatures similar to the terrestrial species shown below).

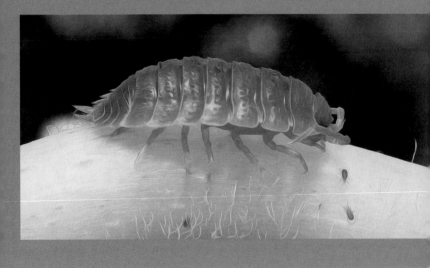

SPECIES: _____   DATE: _____

LOCATION: _____

BAIT: _____

NOTES: _____

_____

_____

_____

SHARKS

Sharks are famous for their cartilaginous bodies, and they are as feared as they are revered. With hundreds of shark species found the world over, sharks range from the tiny dwarf-lantern shark (at just under 8 inches in length) to the massive Great White Shark, which can reach upwards of 30 feet long. (And prehistoric sharks, such as the famous *Megalodon*, were even larger.) Shark attacks on people are incredibly rare, but the attacks that have occurred have been relentlessly publicized—think of the hysteria surrounding the attacks that led to *Jaws*—and this has led shark populations in a steep decline, with many notable species now listed as vulnerable or near-threatened.

SPECIES: DATE:

LOCATION:

BAIT:

NOTES:

SPECIES: DATE:

LOCATION:

BAIT:

NOTES:

SPECIES: DATE:

LOCATION:

BAIT:

NOTES:

SPECIES: DATE:

LOCATION:

BAIT:

NOTES:

SPECIES: DATE:

LOCATION:

BAIT:

NOTES:

SPECIES: DATE:

LOCATION:

BAIT:

NOTES:

SPECIES: DATE:

LOCATION:

BAIT:

NOTES:

SPECIES: DATE:

LOCATION:

BAIT:

NOTES:

SPECIES: DATE:

LOCATION:

BAIT:

NOTES:

SPECIES: DATE:

LOCATION:

BAIT:

NOTES:

SPECIES: _____ DATE: _____

LOCATION: _____

BAIT: _____

NOTES: _____

_____

_____

SPECIES: _____ DATE: _____

LOCATION: _____

BAIT: _____

NOTES: _____

_____

_____

SPECIES: _____ DATE: _____

LOCATION: _____

BAIT: _____

NOTES: _____

_____

_____

SPECIES: _____ DATE: _____

LOCATION: _____

BAIT: _____

NOTES: _____

_____

_____

SPECIES: _____ DATE: _____

LOCATION: _____

BAIT: _____

NOTES: _____

_____

_____

SPECIES: _____   DATE: _____

LOCATION: _____

BAIT: _____

NOTES: _____

_____

_____

_____

SPECIES: _____   DATE: _____

LOCATION: _____

BAIT: _____

NOTES: _____

_____

_____

_____

SPECIES: _____   DATE: _____

LOCATION: _____

BAIT: _____

NOTES: _____

_____

_____

_____

SPECIES: _____   DATE: _____

LOCATION: _____

BAIT: _____

NOTES: _____

_____

_____

_____

SPECIES: _____   DATE: _____

LOCATION: _____

BAIT: _____

NOTES: _____

_____

_____

_____

BIOLUMINESCENCE IN THE MIDNIGHT ZONE

One of the strangest environments on Earth, the Midnight Zone spans from around 3,000 feet deep in the oceans to around 13,000 feet deep. Perpetually shrouded in darkness, it is something of an in-between place. It's too deep to receive direct sunlight, and therefore there are no plants, but fish and other animals do exist. Most are tiny, by the ocean's standards, but studded with teeth, and because there is so little food available in such environments, the animals that live there have remarkable evolutionary adaptations. The famous anglerfish is an example; some deep-sea species feature a lighted "lure" on the head, which attracts other fish because it resembles prey. When they get close enough, the prey is, well, lunch. That's not even the strangest thing about anglerfish. In some species, adult males (which are often unable to hunt on their own) have one job: to find a mate. When they do, they bite into the female, releasing enzymes that fuse the pair physically together. The female effectively feeds the male, and, in return, receives sperm. This is known as sexual symbiosis.

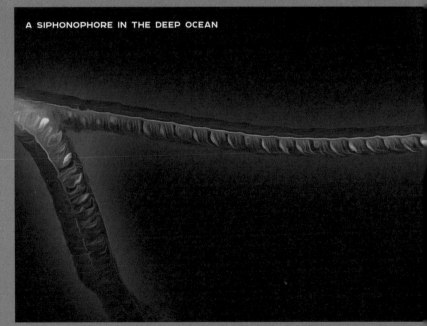

A SIPHONOPHORE IN THE DEEP OCEAN

Image courtesy of NOAA Office of Ocean Exploration and Research

SPECIES: _____ DATE: _____

LOCATION: _____

BAIT: _____

NOTES: _____

_____

_____

_____

SPECIES: _____ DATE: _____

LOCATION: _____

BAIT: _____

NOTES: _____

_____

_____

_____

SPECIES: _____ DATE: _____

LOCATION: _____

BAIT: _____

NOTES: _____

_____

_____

_____

SPECIES: _____ DATE: _____

LOCATION: _____

BAIT: _____

NOTES: _____

_____

_____

_____

SPECIES: _____ DATE: _____

LOCATION: _____

BAIT: _____

NOTES: _____

_____

_____

_____

SPECIES: DATE:

LOCATION:

BAIT:

NOTES:

SPECIES: DATE:

LOCATION:

BAIT:

NOTES:

SPECIES: DATE:

LOCATION:

BAIT:

NOTES:

SPECIES: DATE:

LOCATION:

BAIT:

NOTES:

SPECIES: DATE:

LOCATION:

BAIT:

NOTES:

SPECIES: DATE:

LOCATION:

BAIT:

NOTES:

SPECIES: DATE:

LOCATION:

BAIT:

NOTES:

SPECIES: DATE:

LOCATION:

BAIT:

NOTES:

SPECIES: DATE:

LOCATION:

BAIT:

NOTES:

SPECIES: DATE:

LOCATION:

BAIT:

NOTES:

SPECIES: _____ DATE: _____

LOCATION: _____

BAIT: _____

NOTES: _____

_____

_____

SPECIES: _____ DATE: _____

LOCATION: _____

BAIT: _____

NOTES: _____

_____

_____

BILLFISH

Billfish are among the most famous fish in the sea. They're celebrated for their huge size, athletic jumping ability once hooked, and their pronounced bills that extend well beyond their body. The swordfish and the marlin family are two of the most well-known billfish, but others include sailfish and spearfish. And true to their name, billfish can be potentially dangerous, both in part to their large size and their sharp bills, which can impale anglers that are in the wrong place. In one case in the Atlantic, a marlin that was almost to the boat leapt forward, impaling the would-be angler, who survived. In another, a surf-diver in Hawaii was impaled by the prey he was attempting to spear.

SAILFISH

SPECIES: _____ DATE: _____

LOCATION: _____

BAIT: _____

NOTES: _____

_____

_____

_____

SPECIES: _____ DATE: _____

LOCATION: _____

BAIT: _____

NOTES: _____

_____

_____

_____

SPECIES: _____ DATE: _____

LOCATION: _____

BAIT: _____

NOTES: _____

_____

_____

_____

SPECIES: _____ DATE: _____

LOCATION: _____

BAIT: _____

NOTES: _____

_____

_____

_____

SPECIES: _____ DATE: _____

LOCATION: _____

BAIT: _____

NOTES: _____

_____

_____

_____

SPECIES: _____ DATE: _____

LOCATION: _____

BAIT: _____

NOTES: _____

_____

_____

_____

SPECIES: _____ DATE: _____

LOCATION: _____

BAIT: _____

NOTES: _____

_____

_____

_____

SPECIES: _____ DATE: _____

LOCATION: _____

BAIT: _____

NOTES: _____

_____

_____

_____

SPECIES: _____ DATE: _____

LOCATION: _____

BAIT: _____

NOTES: _____

_____

_____

_____

SPECIES: _____ DATE: _____

LOCATION: _____

BAIT: _____

NOTES: _____

_____

_____

_____

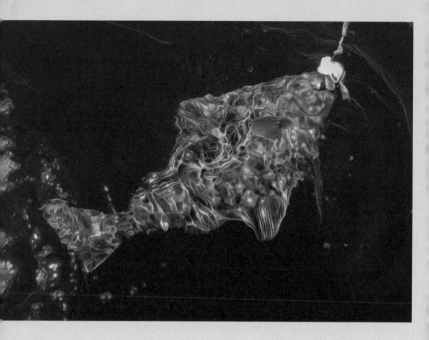

HALIBUT

There are two varieties of halibut, one native to the Atlantic, and one native to the Pacific. Both of these flatfish grow to huge sizes, with exceptional Atlantic halibut reaching more than a dozen feet long and more than 700 pounds in weight. As flatfish, halibut have adapted to residing flat on the ocean floor; their eyes perch out from the top of their head. They don't start that way, though; when they are larvae, they look like normal fish. But as they grow, one eye changes position. In fact, in some flatfish families, the eye heads to the right side of the body (they are known as right-eyed flatfish); in others, known as left-eyed flatfish, they head to the left. Both the Atlantic and Pacific halibut are "right-eyed."

SPECIES: _____   DATE: _____

LOCATION: _____

BAIT: _____

NOTES: _____

_____

_____

_____

SPECIES: _____ DATE: _____

LOCATION: _____

BAIT: _____

NOTES: _____

_____

_____

_____

SPECIES: _____ DATE: _____

LOCATION: _____

BAIT: _____

NOTES: _____

_____

_____

_____

SPECIES: _____ DATE: _____

LOCATION: _____

BAIT: _____

NOTES: _____

_____

_____

_____

SPECIES: _____ DATE: _____

LOCATION: _____

BAIT: _____

NOTES: _____

_____

_____

_____

SPECIES: _____ DATE: _____

LOCATION: _____

BAIT: _____

NOTES: _____

_____

_____

_____

Cover and book design by Jonathan Norberg

Front cover photo: Fish scales background: **Konstanttin/Shutterstock.com**

Back cover photo: Fish scales background: **Konstanttin/Shutterstock.com**; Northern Pike: **Krzysztof Odziomek/Shutterstock.com**); Bluegill Sunfish: **Steven Russell Smith Ohio/Shutterstock.com**; Tarpon: **Miguel Abrams/Shutterstock.com**

Spine photo: Fishing bobber: **Lauren Wilder/Shutterstock.com**

Used under license from Shutterstock.com:

White Sturgeon: **CSNafzger**; Northern Pike: **Peter Toth**; Tarpon: **Diego Grandi**; Walleye: **Piotr Wawrzyniuk**; Largemouth Bass: **Steven Russell Smith Ohio**; Smallmouth Bass: **RLS Photo**; Crappie: **samray**; Tuna: **Al McGashan**; Muskellunge: **M Huston**; Sunfish: **Six Drive**; Yellow Perch: **Nate Allred**; Whale Shark: **Andrea Izzotti**; Least Killfish, Asian Carp: **Vladimir Wrangel**; Fish hook: **Nomad_Soul**; Pro Fishermen: **Steve Bower**; Sea Lamprey: **Maria Dryfhout**; Northern Snakehead: **Realest Nature**; Bullhead: **Jan Mlkvy**; Flathead Catfish: **Kletr**; Bait shop: **Brian S**; Talking fishermen: **RossHelen**; Ninespine Stickleback: **Rudmer Zwerver**; Eating Sea Lamprey: **Vo-Yggdrasill**; Taxidermy: **Noel V. Baebler**; Bass Boat: **Pierre Rebollar**; Fishing equipment: **FedBul**; Lionfish: **bearcreative**; Isopod: **Jeremy A. Casado**; Bull Shark: **Ciurzynski**; Billfish: **FIMP**; Halibut: **Jon C. Beverly**

10 9 8 7 6 5 4 3 2 1

Fishing Journal: Catch 'em and Record 'em
Copyright © 2020 by AdventureKEEN
Published by Adventure Publications
An imprint of AdventureKEEN
330 Garfield Street South
Cambridge, Minnesota 55008
(800) 678-7006
www.adventurepublications.net
Printed in China
ISBN 978-1-59193-952-8 (pbk.)